THE FOUNDER FIT

Finding the Business Idea That's Right for You

www.thefounderfit.com

Ike Eze

The Founder Fit: Finding the Business Idea That's Right for You

Copyright © 2025 Ike Eze

Published by **Knomaad LLC**
First Edition

For inquiries, visit www.thefounderfit.com

CONTENTS

FOREWORD

Every great business starts with an idea—but discovering the right idea is often the biggest challenge. Throughout my decades as an entrepreneur, founder, and investor, I've witnessed firsthand the immense ambition of business owners. Many had the drive, the talent, and the hunger for success, yet they kept coming back to the same fundamental question: **"How do I figure out the right idea for me for a business?"**

This question is deceptively simple, yet its answer holds the key to sustainable growth, lasting impact, and true fulfillment in entrepreneurship. Some founders stumble upon their ideas through sheer luck or circumstance, while others spend months—sometimes years—searching for clarity. Seeing this struggle across so many conversations inspired me to develop a methodology—a structured approach that simplifies the process of uncovering, evaluating, and refining business ideas. Whether you're starting from scratch or acquiring an existing company, this book is designed to serve as a guide, helping entrepreneurs and business owners turn uncertainty into opportunity.

The journey to writing this book wasn't one I initially planned. For years, I had carried these insights in discussions, mentoring sessions, and personal notes, never quite taking the step to transform them into a full-fledged manuscript. Then, inspiration struck from an unexpected source—my younger sister, Napa. An avid reader and an aspiring novelist, she made the decision to write her first fiction book and self-publish it. Witnessing her unwavering dedication sparked something in me. Without realizing it, she gave me the push I needed to finally put my thoughts into words, turning decades of knowledge into a resource that can empower others.

No book comes to life without support, and I am deeply grateful to those who made this possible. My executive assistant, Blessing, played a crucial role in removing obstacles, ensuring that I had the time, focus, and space to bring this vision to completion. My children—Adamma, Ikem, and Oluchi—along with my wife, Yvy, have been my foundation, continually pushing me toward growth and improvement, both professionally and personally. Their belief in me is a constant source of motivation.

Entrepreneurship is not merely about launching companies—it's about transformation, both in business and in self. If you're here searching for your next big idea, I hope this book provides clarity, confidence, and actionable steps to shape your future. The right idea is out there—waiting to be discovered, refined, and brought to life. Let's get started.

Ike Eze

Entrepreneur, Investor, and Author

INTRODUCTION

This book stems from decades of guiding entrepreneurs and business owners through the process of developing new ventures or acquiring existing ones. Over the years, the same core questions have emerged repeatedly. To avoid reiterating the same advice in one-on-one sessions, I've compiled my process here, for anyone to use.

Choosing the right business idea is crucial, and this book addresses three key aspects:

- Why the right business matters.
- The dangers of pursuing the wrong business.
- How this book helps you identify your ideal business.

First, choosing the right business idea matters because time is precious. Wasting it is the worst mistake, especially for entrepreneurs, for whom timing can be everything. Opportunities vanish when their window closes. Life itself is time-sensitive, and years spent on a failing business are irretrievable. Careful preliminary assessment, thoughtful consideration, and strategic planning can prevent many errors and save significant time.

For example, don't pursue real estate simply because it worked for friends. You might discover that your strengths lie in online marketing, making an e-commerce drop-shipping business a better fit. The wrong initial choice wastes valuable time. Avoiding this waste is a primary goal.

I hope this book helps you minimize wasted time.

The second key consideration is actually starting. Many great ideas die with the people who conceived them. The clock is always ticking. It's essential to begin implementing an idea, even if it fails. At least it was given a chance. Small beginnings are fine; the key is to be on the right track. Momentum builds as you progress. Your ambitions will expand year by year. Looking back, you'll often be surprised at the scale of what you've built from those small beginnings.

Third, choosing the right idea is essential because the entrepreneurial journey is inevitably difficult. You'll need a strong connection to your idea to persevere. If you lack that alignment, you're more likely to give up prematurely. Early failures can also create fear of future attempts, preventing you from re-entering the entrepreneurial arena.

In essence:

1. Choose the right idea to avoid wasting time.
2. Start with the right idea, no matter how small.
3. Align with your idea; passion will fuel your perseverance through challenges, allowing you to adapt and succeed.

Many potentially successful ideas align uniquely with your skills, capabilities, and interests.

Part 1 of this book guides you through a self-assessment to identify your strengths, desires, and perspectives.

Part 2 helps you look outward, examining business ideas in the market. The goal is to match validated business ideas with your personal strengths and outlook.

Finally, Part 3 focuses on narrowing down and testing your best ideas. After the inward self-assessment and the outward market analysis, you'll combine them to refine your options, test them, and move forward. Additionally, you will have a 28-day plan and explore the distinction between entrepreneurship and business ownership.

The distinction between an entrepreneur and a business owner is essential in determining if you are geared for one path over the other.

This book will greatly assist in working through self-discovery, matching that to business ideas and implementing action. Diligently follow the steps and you will arrive safely at the right port.

PART 1

LOOKING INWARD –
FINDING IDEAS THROUGH SELF-DISCOVERY

Matching Your Strengths and Passions to the Right Business

Many economists and business leaders say that following your passion is a mistake. They point out that many fortunes are made in "unsexy" businesses, and successful people often advise *against* pursuing your passion.

While there's some truth to this, there's also truth in focusing on what you're passionate about. Perhaps "interest" is a better word here. Starting a viable company is challenging and remains so for a long time. If you're not interested in the business, you won't have the drive to push through. Some level of interest—curiosity, engagement, or passion—is crucial for success.

Why Choosing the Right Business Idea Matters

The ideal scenario is when your natural capabilities and accumulated experience align with your interests. While this may not always be achievable, it's a worthwhile goal.

Identify what you're both good at and passionate about. This is the first step: understanding that passion alone isn't enough, but it still matters. The second step is identifying your core skills and expertise, which is crucial for avoiding failure.

For example, someone seeking cash flow might consider buying a laundromat: a self-service facility with washers and dryers. The owner's responsibilities include collecting cash, emptying trash, cleaning, checking drains, advertising, and maintaining the lighting. This business demands daily physical tasks. If you prefer a virtual lifestyle and dislike leaving the house, a laundromat is a poor fit. It can be a good business, but it might not be the right business *for you*.

Similarly, an online advertising business requires customer interaction, sales outreach, and building a portfolio of testimonials. If you dislike these activities or are unwilling to learn them, you'll struggle to acquire customers, and the business will likely fail. You must align your skills with the business's requirements.

Or, if you want to build a FinTech company but lack technical skills and are unwilling to learn the basics, you'll face challenges. While you might find a technical co-founder, they may not have the specific expertise needed for your tech stack or the financial services industry. This can lead to a steep learning curve and a series of unsuitable co-founder relationships. Domain knowledge is essential here. A lack of interest in gaining that knowledge will create a rocky start.

The Dangers of Jumping into the Wrong Business

Jumping into a business you're ill-equipped for leads to a learning curve that consumes time and money.

Consider the real estate example again. Your realtor friends have extensive knowledge of listings, lead generation, distressed property acquisition, banking relationships, and marketing. As an accountant, you see their attractive numbers and believe you can replicate their success immediately. However, you lack their domain knowledge, acquired through experience or education. This knowledge gap creates a learning curve that costs time and money. Entering the wrong business without accounting for this curve puts you at a significant disadvantage.

Another danger is unassessed risk. Planning allows you to evaluate potential risks. In one early startup, we explored building voice-activated scheduling software. But in those pre-internet days, distribution through retail computer stores was a major hurdle. We lacked experience in that area, and the challenge of securing shelf space and differentiating ourselves was daunting. The learning curve was steep, and after assessing the risks, we pivoted to a more suitable opportunity.

A third danger is a lack of resources (money, time, people, information, distribution, partnerships, etc.). A viable business idea requires resources. While you won't excel in every area, assessing your resource needs is crucial. A lack of critical resources, such as the cash needed to build a factory, can prevent your idea from ever becoming a reality. You'll need to determine how to mitigate this risk (e.g., through loans or investors) or choose a different path.

A fourth danger of entering the wrong business is early failure, which can be devastating to your entrepreneurial spirit. This book aims to help you identify the right ideas and markets, minimizing the risk of early failure. While external factors like economic downturns or unforeseen events (like COVID-19) can cause failure, we're focused on mitigating *idiosyncratic* risks—those specific to your situation.

With that in mind, this book is divided into three parts. The first part focuses on self-discovery to find ideas that fit *you* as an individual with unique needs, perspectives, and skills. We often treat business ideas as universally applicable, but they're not.

How This Book Will Help You Find Your Ideal Business

To understand your strengths and passions, we'll do an exercise: listing what you love and what you're good at. For example, you might list: "I love sales," "I love meeting new people," "I love overcoming challenges," "I love being on the road," and "I love talking to customers to solve their problems." Or, "I love reports," "I love hitting targets," and "I love moving people through the sales funnel." Or, "I like driving and delivering things, interacting with people, and hearing their stories."

List *everything* you like, even if it's 10 or 50 items. Then, rank them from 1 to 5: 1 for "don't like at all" (and that shouldn't be on your list) to 5 for "love it; can't imagine doing anything else." The goal is to identify the top 10 to 15 items that you either love (4 or 5 ranking) *or* are very skilled at.

Avoiding the "Shiny Object" Syndrome

Finally, avoid the "shiny object" syndrome. Just because a friend is successful in real estate or FinTech, that doesn't mean it's right for you. Don't be swayed by hype, whether from the media or your social circle. This chapter emphasizes understanding your own strengths, passions, interests, and desires, and then quantifying them.

Assessing Your Resources and Constraints

U nderstanding your resources and constraints is crucial for evaluating the feasibility of a business idea. It defines the boundaries within which your idea can develop. For instance, starting an airline requires significant capital for aircraft.

However, you could begin with chartered flights, where customers prepay, and gradually expand into a full-fledged airline. Assessing your resources and constraints allows you to create a logical, step-by-step plan, rather than attempting to immediately purchase an Airbus 320. This chapter will explore these resources and constraints.

Time: How Much Can You Realistically Commit?

Time is a critical resource and constraint. Many people want to pursue new business ideas while maintaining the security of their current jobs. However, their job schedules, including commute and work hours, may leave limited time for other pursuits. It's essential to be realistic about your time constraints.

Some individuals have more flexible schedules, such as those who work from home. They may have the ability to multitask or dedicate more time to their business idea. Others may choose to commit to their idea full-time. When assessing time commitment, consider your work schedule, commute, family obligations, and other responsibilities to determine the actual time you can dedicate.

When I started my first company, I meticulously analyzed my schedule, including time for work, commuting, socializing, friends, TV, and phone calls. I realized that my active social life consumed a significant portion of my time. To address this, I relocated to the suburbs to minimize distractions. I also disconnected my phones and sold my TV. This allowed me to shift my focus from socializing on evenings and weekends to dedicating that time to my business idea, before eventually quitting my job to pursue it full-time.

Consider whether you can commit to your business idea full-time, part-time, on evenings and weekends, or only ad hoc.

For example, a person I knew enjoyed making Belgian waffles and wanted to open a kitchen. However, they had a full-time corporate job and preferred a more flexible arrangement. They chose to operate a food truck on weekends, generating a monthly income of $2,000 to $3,000. This allowed them to pursue their passion for cooking without the demands of a full-time restaurant business. By recognizing their time constraints, they found a business model that worked for them.

Money: Bootstrapping vs. External Funding

The second constraint is money. The options range from bootstrapping (self-funding) to seeking external funding. It's important to consider your financial perspective before you commit to a specific business idea. Instead of thinking, "I want to buy an airplane, but can't afford it, so I need external funding," consider your general approach to funding.

There are three main financial situations:

1. **No personal investment:** In this scenario, you commit no personal funds. Business ideas are typically limited to consulting, outsourcing, projects, or contracts. However, this situation can evolve as you generate capital.

2. **Some personal investment:** This involves putting some of your own money into the business. Examples include e-commerce reselling on Instagram (requiring funds for inventory and photography) or starting a photography business (requiring investment in a camera and equipment).

3. **Other people's money:** This can come from family, friends, or investors, usually in the form of equity (ownership in

your company) or debt (loans from banks or financial institutions). Airlines and capital-intensive businesses like real estate, trucking, or manufacturing typically rely on external funding.

Skills: What You Know vs. What You Need to Learn

The third constraint is skills: what you already know versus what you need to learn. In Chapter 1, we discussed identifying your existing skills. For example, realtors seeking to start their own firm possess skills in finding properties, attracting clients, negotiating deals, and building networks.

However, they may lack the skills needed for a FinTech startup, such as coding, product development, marketing, customer acquisition, regulatory compliance, legal knowledge, partner management, and fundraising. It's essential to identify the skills required for your chosen þusiness idea and determine whether you possess them or need to acquire them.

We will address this task in more detail once you have a specific business idea. If your idea requires skills you don't have, you must either discard the idea or determine how to bridge the skills gap.

Risk Tolerance: How Much Uncertainty Can You Handle?

The fourth constraint is risk tolerance: how much uncertainty you can handle. Instead of broadly assessing your risk tolerance, it's more helpful to consider the pressures you'll face. We'll examine three scenarios:

- **Low risk:** You are the only one dependent on the business's success. If you get a contract or customer, that's great, but if you don't, your basic needs are still met.
- **Medium risk:** Other people depend on your business for their income. You must generate sufficient revenue to pay them on time, or they may face financial hardship.
- **High risk:** You are responsible to both employees and investors who have put their savings into your venture. You must allocate capital wisely to generate returns and pay salaries.

Therefore, when evaluating risk tolerance, consider whether your business idea involves low, medium, or high risk, based on the level of dependency on its success.

Defining Your Ideal Business Lifestyle

Many people consider their desired lifestyle *after* achieving business success. However, it's more effective to define your ideal lifestyle *before* starting a business. The way you run your business in its early stages will likely mirror how you run it when it's successful. For example, a factory owner who is deeply involved in daily production will likely remain so even after the factory becomes successful.

While there might be a transition period, a significant shift in lifestyle post-success is uncommon and can sometimes lead to business decline. Therefore, this chapter will help you define your ideal business lifestyle from the outset.

Do You Want Freedom, Wealth, Impact, or Something Else?

It's essential to determine your primary motivation. There's no right or wrong answer, but clarity is crucial. Do you envision a lifestyle of freedom, working remotely from a beach, or a demanding schedule in a high-production environment? Understanding your preference—freedom, wealth, impact, or something else—will guide your choices.

- **Freedom:** This might involve working from a laptop in a beach town, allowing for travel and leisure.
- **Wealth:** This goal requires business ideas with the potential for substantial financial gain.
- **Impact:** This involves a desire to improve the world, whether through education, addressing hunger, or providing affordable housing.

Ultimately, you define your own path. Identifying your core desire will help you stay focused and committed.

Location Independence vs. Local Brick-and-Mortar

Another key consideration is location. Do you want a business that allows you to work from anywhere, or one that requires a fixed location? This involves a spectrum:

- **No fixed location:** This offers maximum flexibility. For example, a consultant could work with clients globally while living anywhere.

- **Regional presence:** This involves some connection to a specific area, without requiring constant presence. Examples include real estate investors who visit their properties periodically, or e-commerce businesses that can be operated from various locations.
- **Fixed location:** This demands a physical presence. Examples include logistics companies, dry cleaners, retail stores, and hair salons. These businesses require consistent on-site management.

You must decide whether you want a location-independent business, a business with a regional presence, or a traditional brick-and-mortar establishment.

Scalability: Lifestyle Business vs. High-Growth Startup

Consider how scalable you want your business to be. Do you want a lifestyle business or a high-growth startup? High-growth startups exist in many sectors, not just technology.

A helpful exercise is to imagine yourself describing your business in three years. Do you talk about your personal experiences and travels (lifestyle business), or are you constantly promoting your business and its potential impact (high-growth startup)?

People pursuing lifestyle businesses tend to focus on their personal experiences, while those building high-growth companies are driven to convert others to their vision.

- **Lifestyle businesses:** These typically aim to generate a specific income to support a desired lifestyle.
- **High-growth startups:** These seek maximum expansion and market dominance.

There's a general correlation between the desire for freedom and lifestyle businesses, and between the pursuit of wealth and high-growth businesses. Understanding your own inclinations will help you make informed decisions.

Aligning Business Choices with Personal Goals

Defining your ideal business lifestyle can reveal conflicting desires. For instance, wanting a high-growth company with low risk and significant personal freedom presents a challenge, as high growth typically involves high risk and intense commitment.

Similarly, combining location independence with a traditional retail storefront is difficult. The management demands of a fixed-location business can conflict with the desire for a flexible, location-independent lifestyle.

This initial self-assessment involves understanding your desired activities, location, skills, expertise, business scale, lifestyle, and financial and time commitments. Once you have a clear understanding of these factors, you'll be ready to move on to the next stage.

PART 2

LOOKING OUTWARD –
VALIDATING BUSINESS IDEAS
IN THE MARKET

Spotting Market Gaps and Trends

In this fourth chapter, we will delve into the crucial skill of identifying market gaps and understanding prevailing trends. This ability is fundamental for anyone seeking to launch a successful business, as it allows you to position your venture in areas with unmet needs or significant growth potential.

How to Identify Underserved Markets

One of the most effective ways to uncover promising business opportunities is by identifying underserved markets. As individuals navigating our daily lives, we are constantly exposed to a multitude of situations and interactions, presenting us with a unique vantage point for observation. We encounter inefficiencies, frustrations, and unmet needs, often without consciously recognizing their potential as business opportunities. The key capability we must cultivate is the disciplined practice of documenting the problems we observe in our everyday experiences. We literally walk by potential business ideas on a regular basis.

I recall an exercise from my university engineering program that profoundly shaped my approach to problem identification. In our final year, faced with the daunting task of selecting a capstone project, our professor offered a simple yet powerful technique: we were instructed to carry a notebook and diligently record every problem we encountered. Subsequently, during moments of quiet reflection, we would revisit these recorded issues and contemplate potential solutions. The remarkable benefit of this method was that it broadened our minds beyond purely engineering challenges to encompass the everyday frustrations and inconveniences we all face.

By consistently writing down these seemingly mundane problems, we began to recognize patterns and areas where existing solutions were inadequate or absent. Furthermore, during our brainstorming sessions, we discovered that these problems could be addressed through diverse approaches – some requiring technical innovations, others process improvements, some necessitating policy changes, and still others demanding creative marketing strategies. This exercise effectively trained our minds to operate within a problem-solution framework, a crucial mindset for any aspiring entrepreneur.

Therefore, the practical exercise we will undertake is to emulate this approach in our daily lives. Utilize your smartphone, a dedicated notebook, or a digital note-taking application like Notion to meticulously record every problem you encounter as you go about your day. The immediacy of the problem is paramount; the fresher the observation, the more accurate and insightful your note will be. Avoid the temptation to immediately jump to a solution. The process should be sequential: first, diligently document the problem itself, and second, separately engage in the creative process of devising potential solutions.

Over the course of the next few days, perhaps extending to a couple of weeks, your sole focus should be on capturing a comprehensive list of problems you observe. Then, during your dedicated quiet time, you can begin to explore potential solutions for these identified issues. The outcome of this exercise will be a valuable compilation of problems, with a subset potentially accompanied by initial solution ideas. This collection will serve as the foundational material for filtering and refining your business concepts. We will subsequently analyze this list to determine which problems align best with your unique skills, experiences, and passions, effectively guiding you toward identifying genuine gaps and underserved markets. The essence of this process lies in the simple yet powerful act of consistently documenting the problems we encounter in our daily lives.

Emerging Trends vs. Fading Industries

Another critical aspect of spotting market gaps and trends involves discerning between emerging trends that offer significant growth potential and fading industries that may present limited opportunities or require a niche strategy. It's crucial to recognize that building a sustainable business takes time and effort, and aligning your venture with the right market segment is paramount for long-term success.

Consider the energy sector as an example. If your analysis suggests that the traditional energy sector is not experiencing significant growth, but you are drawn to a lifestyle business model, an interesting niche might exist in providing specialized maintenance supplies, such as high-durability bolts for the flanges in oil pipelines. Despite the broader industry trends, this specific product caters to a consistent need within the existing infrastructure. While the oil industry might eventually decline over the very long term, it will likely continue to require maintenance and support services for decades to come, potentially offering a stable, albeit not rapidly growing, business opportunity. This illustrates a scenario where a business operates within a fading industry but addresses a persistent and essential need.

Conversely, consider the market for ringtones. This industry has largely faded with the advent of sophisticated smartphones and alternative forms of personalization. Attempting to build a significant business in ringtones today would likely be a challenging endeavor, as the market is shrinking, lacks substantial consumer demand,

and does not attract the attention of major telecommunications companies, making market penetration exceedingly difficult. This exemplifies the risk of pursuing opportunities in a clearly fading industry.

However, it's important to acknowledge that individuals with deep, insider knowledge of a particular fading industry might still identify unique and profitable niche opportunities that are not apparent to outsiders. Their understanding of specific pain points or underserved sub-segments within the declining market can be invaluable.

Let's now focus on emerging trends. When we think of emerging trends, the technology sector often comes to mind, as it is frequently at the forefront of innovation and the creation of new markets poised for rapid expansion. Understanding how to identify an emerging trend typically involves a degree of postulation and synthesis. It's about observing existing trends, often in seemingly disparate areas, and combining them to anticipate the emergence of new market opportunities.

The story of Uber provides a compelling illustration of this concept. The founders recognized two key emerging trends: the increasing ubiquity and capability of smartphones, particularly the development of app stores that allowed for the distribution of software applications, and the maturation of digital mapping platforms, specifically Google Maps, which offered API access for integrating mapping functionality into other applications. By synthesizing these two trends – the proliferation of powerful mobile devices and the availability of accurate and comprehensive digital maps – the opportunity for on-demand ride-hailing services emerged. Ride-hailing was not a pre-existing market; it was a novel opportunity born from the convergence of these two significant technological advancements. This demonstrates the power of identifying and combining emerging trends to create entirely new business categories.

We can apply a similar paradigm of assessment to other areas. For example, consider the intersection of increasing smartphone penetration in Africa, projected to reach a significant milestone within the next five years, and the ongoing evolution towards simpler and more seamless on- and off-ramping of digital currencies. Currently, interacting with digital currencies often requires a degree of technical sophistication, involving digital wallets, private keys, and various security protocols. This complex infrastructure is reminiscent of the early days of the internet, where users needed modems, dial-up connections, and specialized software like CompuServe or AOL to access the online world.

The widespread adoption of the internet was largely facilitated by the simplification of access. Telecommunications companies and browser developers eliminated the technical barriers, making it as easy as turning on a device and connecting wirelessly. Similarly, simplifying the process of converting between traditional and digital currencies could unlock significant opportunities, particularly in regions with high mobile penetration. By observing these two converging trends – increased smartphone usage and simplified digital currency access – we can begin to envision potential emerging opportunities in areas like mobile payments, cross-border transactions, and digital financial services tailored to the African market.

A more immediate example of converging trends can be seen in the context of international trade. The projected increase in US tariffs on imported goods in the near future will likely make these goods more expensive for American consumers. Simultaneously, manufacturers in other parts of the world who previously relied heavily on the US market will be actively seeking new markets for their products. The convergence of these two trends – reduced access to the US market and the need for alternative markets – creates potential opportunities in areas such as international trade consulting, facilitating new supply chain routes, and identifying emerging consumer markets for these displaced goods. This is a non-technical opportunity driven by evolving global trade dynamics.

Another related consideration involves tariffs on food stocks. If tariffs on food inputs increase in the US, domestically processed foods using these inputs may become less competitive. This could create opportunities for processing these same agricultural goods in other regions without such tariffs and then exporting the finished products to the US or other markets. This represents a potential processing and logistics opportunity, although it may be more capital-intensive. However, for individuals with expertise in international trade, opportunities may exist in sourcing and trading these commodities without the need for significant capital investment in processing facilities.

Shifting our focus to fading industries, these opportunities are often best recognized by individuals with deep experience and understanding within those sectors. They possess insights into specific unmet needs or inefficiencies that may not be obvious to outsiders. For instance, the global push towards electric vehicles (EVs) is a well-known trend. However, this also creates opportunities in related, potentially fading, industries. Many individuals will continue to own and maintain gasoline-powered vehicles, especially classic cars. This presents opportunities for businesses offering conversion kits to alternative fuels like CNG (Compressed Natural Gas), which burns cleaner than traditional gasoline or diesel.

Furthermore, the transition to EVs, with their focus on battery technology and onboard electronics, may lead to a decline in the demand for traditional mechanical car parts. This creates an emerging need for robust and cost-effective manufacturing of replacement parts for older vehicles. Businesses with advanced 3D printing capabilities for both plastics and metals, capable of producing parts that meet the demanding specifications of automotive applications, could capitalize on this evolving landscape.

In summary, identifying opportunities in emerging trends often involves creative synthesis and a broad awareness of technological and societal shifts. Conversely, opportunities in fading industries are typically best identified by those with deep domain expertise and a nuanced understanding of the remaining needs within those markets.

The "Scratch Your Own Itch" Approach

Another significant approach to spotting market gaps and trends is what is commonly referred to as the "scratch your own itch" method. This involves identifying a problem that you personally experience and developing a solution to address it. The underlying assumption is that if you, as a consumer within a specific segment, encounter this problem, there are likely other individuals within that same segment who experience a similar pain point and would therefore benefit from your solution.

While this approach has led to the creation of many successful products and services, it's crucial to be aware of a potential pitfall: the assumption that your problem is shared by a large enough market to sustain a viable business. Your specific needs or the way you experience a particular problem might be quite unique, and the number of people who approach it in the same way might be smaller than you initially believe. While a market may indeed exist, its size might not be as substantial as your initial assumptions. Numerous excellent products have emerged from individuals solving their own problems, but market validation is critical to ensure its commercial viability.

Once you have identified potential trends and problems, a crucial step is to expand your understanding and uncover related or less obvious opportunities. A valuable way to extend this discovery process is through diligent research. Utilize tools like Google Trends to identify trending search terms and topics, explore relevant subreddits on

Reddit to gauge public sentiment and identify recurring issues, and participate in industry-specific forums to understand the challenges and needs of professionals in those fields.

The overarching objective is to engage in broad and consistent reading, consuming information from diverse sources to identify patterns, and infer potential emerging opportunities that may not be immediately apparent. A highly effective technique is to identify two seemingly undeniable trends within the same industry and then consider their convergence. By asking the question, "If Trend A continues to hold true, and Trend B also progresses as expected, what new possibilities or needs might emerge from their intersection?" you can proactively identify novel business opportunities with significant potential.

Analyzing Competition and Demand

T his chapter delves into the critical aspects of analyzing competition and demand, essential steps for anyone venturing into a new business or seeking to expand an existing one. A thorough understanding of the competitive landscape and the dynamics of market demand can significantly improve the chances of success and mitigate potential risks.

How to Research Competitors (Without Getting Discouraged)

The initial phase of exploring any business idea involves researching existing competitors. This step is crucial for gaining insights into the current market landscape, identifying potential challenges, and discovering opportunities for differentiation. A common practice is to use search engines like Google or AI-powered tools such as DeepSea, ChatGPT, or Perplexity to identify firms and entrepreneurs operating in the same or adjacent spaces.

The primary objective of this competitive research is to thoroughly investigate these companies and their solutions. By understanding their offerings, target audience, marketing strategies, and overall business model, you can discern valuable information. You might discover that while these competitors operate in the same general space, their specific focus or approach differs from your proposed idea. Alternatively, you might find direct competitors offering similar solutions, but with potential weaknesses or areas where your approach could be superior.

It's important not to become discouraged when you find that others are already pursuing similar ventures. This is a natural part of the research process. Instead, view this information as valuable data that can inform your strategy. If the competitive landscape appears too crowded and you don't believe you can effectively compete, it might be wise to pivot your idea or explore alternative market segments. This proactive approach can save you significant time and resources in the long run.

However, if your research reveals a specific niche or a differentiated approach that existing competitors are not addressing, this could indicate a viable opportunity. As you continue your research, focus on identifying these areas of differentiation and assessing their potential for success. Remember that thorough and ongoing research is a cornerstone of sound business decision-making.

Signs of a Saturated Market vs. Untapped Potential

Understanding the difference between a saturated market and one with untapped potential is crucial for determining the viability of a business idea. Market saturation, while not inherently negative, signifies a specific set of conditions that can significantly impact a new entrant's ability to compete and succeed. Recognizing these signs early on can help you make informed decisions about whether to proceed with an idea, modify it, or explore alternative opportunities.

Here are some key indicators of a saturated market:

- **Too many competitors:** A large number of companies offering similar products or services, with little to no differentiation, is a classic sign of saturation. This creates a highly competitive environment where it's difficult for new entrants to stand out.
- **Shrinking margins and price wars:** When a market's growth slows, companies often resort to price competition to gain market share. This leads to shrinking profit margins and intense price wars, making it challenging for new businesses with fewer resources to compete.

- **Low customer loyalty:** In saturated markets, customers often have numerous options with minimal differences between them. This results in low customer loyalty, as consumers can easily switch to a competitor offering a slightly lower price or a minor variation of the product.

- **Decline or flat growth:** A market that is declining or experiencing flat growth indicates that it has likely reached its peak. In such markets, the major players have already established themselves, and opportunities for new entrants are limited.

- **High customer acquisition costs:** As a market becomes more crowded, the cost of acquiring new customers tends to increase significantly. Established players have already built brand recognition and customer relationships, making it expensive for new entrants to compete for attention. For example, the cost-per-click for online advertising in certain saturated markets can be extremely high, making it difficult for new companies to gain traction.

- **Slow innovation, little differentiation:** In a saturated market, most of the significant innovations have already occurred. New developments tend to be incremental and offer little differentiation, making it difficult for new entrants to disrupt the status quo.

- **Consolidation of markets:** Market consolidation, through mergers and acquisitions, is a common sign of saturation. Companies seek to increase market share and improve efficiency by acquiring competitors, leading to fewer players and reduced opportunities for new entrants.

- **Customer overwhelm:** When customers are faced with an overwhelming number of choices, it becomes increasingly difficult for a new business to capture their attention. Cutting through the clutter and effectively communicating a unique value proposition is a significant challenge in a saturated market.

- **Regulations and barriers to entry:** Governments may introduce regulations to limit consolidation and maintain competition in saturated markets. Additionally, high barriers to entry, such as substantial capital requirements, distribution challenges, or proprietary technology, can make it difficult for new companies to enter the market. For instance, establishing a new chip fabrication plant requires an enormous capital investment, creating a significant barrier to entry.

Despite these challenges, saturated markets can still present opportunities for those who can identify and exploit specific niches. Consider the hotel industry, which is dominated by major players like Hilton and Sheraton. While the overall market might seem saturated, Airbnb successfully carved out a niche by offering travelers unique lodging experiences with a focus on control, choice, and personalized stays. By redefining the industry and focusing on a specific customer segment, Airbnb was able to thrive in a seemingly saturated market.

Untapped Potential Markets

In contrast to saturated markets, untapped potential markets offer significant opportunities for growth and expansion. These markets are characterized by unmet needs, emerging trends, and a lack of dominant players. Recognizing the signs of an untapped market can provide a significant first-mover advantage.

Here are some key indicators of an untapped potential market:

- **High demand, low supply:** When there is a strong demand for a particular product or service but the existing supply is insufficient to meet that demand, it indicates an untapped market. This situation often arises when the existing players are focused on their core businesses and have not yet recognized the potential of this underserved segment.

- **Rapidly growing audience or trends:** Identifying emerging trends and predicting future market directions can reveal untapped potential. By synthesizing multiple trends, you can anticipate the needs of a rapidly growing audience and position your business to capitalize on that growth.

- **Frustration with current options:** When customers express dissatisfaction or frustration with the existing solutions in a market, it signals an unmet need and an opportunity for innovation. Businesses that can effectively address these frustrations have a high potential for success.

- **Underserved demographics:** Markets that have been neglected or ignored by existing players often represent untapped potential. This can occur when the revenue per customer in a particular demographic is lower than in the markets currently served by incumbents. New entrants can often succeed by replicating existing solutions at a lower cost, making the underserved market viable.

- **No clear market leader:** In emerging markets where no single company has established dominance, there is significant room for new players to enter and gain market share. The absence of a clear leader suggests that the market is still evolving and offers opportunities for those who can effectively capture the growing demand.

- **High willingness to pay for a better option:** When potential customers express a willingness to pay a premium for a superior solution to their existing problems, it indicates a strong potential market. Entrepreneurs should pay close attention to such feedback, as it validates the existence of a demand for improved offerings.

- **New tech or behavior makes new solutions possible:** Disruptive technologies or shifts in consumer behavior can create entirely new markets or transform existing ones. Identifying these changes and developing innovative solutions can lead to significant opportunities. For example, the advent of smartphones and mobile data revolutionized numerous industries, from cameras and portable music to ride-hailing and social media.

- **Adjacent market success:** Observing the success of a product or service in a related market can provide insights into untapped potential. If a particular solution is thriving in one geographic region or industry, it might indicate an opportunity to introduce a similar offering in a new market. For instance, the widespread adoption of facial recognition technology in China has opened up new possibilities in areas such as keyless entry, automated check-in/check-out, and contactless payments, suggesting potential opportunities in other markets.

- **Sector with low marketing noise:** A market with a viable solution but low marketing activity may indicate an untapped opportunity. This could be due to the newness of the solution or the lack of resources among existing providers. Businesses that can effectively market their offerings in such sectors may be able to capture a significant share of the market.

When Low Competition Niches Are Worth It

A low-competition niche can be an attractive opportunity, but it is essential to evaluate its potential carefully. While the lack of competitors might seem appealing, it's crucial to determine whether the niche is genuinely promising or simply unattractive to others for valid reasons.

Here are some factors that indicate a low-competition niche might be worth pursuing:

- **Clear demand:** Even if the market is small, there should be clear evidence of demand for a solution. If the existing audience is engaged and underserved, it suggests that the market has the potential to grow.

- **Efficient monetization:** If customers are willing to pay for a solution and the market can be reached cost-effectively, the niche can be profitable.

- Potential for dominance and loyalty: A low-competition niche offers the opportunity to become the go-to brand and build strong customer loyalty.

- **Market growth potential:** The niche may be experiencing low competition simply because it is an emerging market that hasn't yet attracted the attention of larger players.

- **Unique suitability:** You might possess unique knowledge, experience, or access that gives you a significant advantage over potential competitors.

- Conversely, here are some reasons why a low-competition niche might not be worth pursuing:

- **No real demand:** The niche might be a dead end with little to no interest from a broader audience.

- **Unworkable unit economics:** The fundamental economics of delivering a product or service in that niche might not be viable.

- **Difficulty in reaching the audience:** The target audience might be fragmented, offline, or expensive to reach, making it difficult to scale the business.

- **Inability to scale:** Even if the business is successful in the niche, there might be no clear path to expand or grow beyond that initial segment.

Using Google Trends, Reddit, and Forums for Research

To effectively analyze competition and demand, it's essential to utilize available research tools. Google Trends, Reddit, and online forums can provide valuable insights into market trends, customer sentiment, and competitive activity. Additionally, reading widely and staying informed about industry developments can help you identify potential opportunities and threats. By combining these research methods, you can develop a comprehensive understanding of the market and make more informed business decisions.

Talking to Potential Customers

Many businesses and entrepreneurs neglect talking to potential customers, which is a critical mistake. It's a common misconception that customer interaction equates to conducting extensive surveys with hundreds of participants. This view is incorrect. In reality, speaking with just five to ten customers can provide valuable insights into what's working, what isn't, and whether your current direction is appropriate.

Entrepreneurs often make critical errors in this phase, which we will address to establish a process for gathering reliable information and advancing your business idea.

Why Assumptions Kill Businesses

A key issue is understanding how assumptions can undermine a business. Entrepreneurs frequently make assumptions, jumping to conclusions without validating them with customer feedback. Here's why relying on assumptions is detrimental:

- **Building the wrong product:** Assuming you understand the product better than your customers can lead to developing something that doesn't meet market needs. Direct customer feedback is essential, and even insights from a small group of five people are more valuable than extensive speculation.

- **Wasting resources:** Investing heavily in development without validating key factors like demand, pricing, customer acquisition costs, and distribution channels can waste significant resources. The more you build on untested assumptions, the more challenging it becomes to pivot if those assumptions are wrong.

- **Not targeting the real problem:** You might optimize a feature that is not a priority for your target audience. As Henry Ford noted, customers might ask for "a faster horse" when the real need is speed. Understanding the core problem (e.g., the need for speed in transportation, rather than a specific vehicle) is crucial.

- **You are not the customer:** Building a product solely for yourself is risky. While it can work if you represent a larger, underserved group, it's essential to validate this assumption by talking to potential customers.

- **Misjudging the market:** Assuming demand exists without verifying it can lead to problems if the market is saturated, too niche, uninterested, or shifting. For example, developing a rotary phone when the market has moved to digital, portable handsets demonstrates a failure to recognize market trends. Additionally, you may overestimate what customers are willing to pay.

- **Not understanding that distribution is king:** Many founders believe that a great product will sell itself. However, poor marketing and distribution are common causes of business failure. It's essential to focus on how to get the product into customers' hands and create a compelling narrative around it.

The solution to these problems is to engage with potential users even before you begin building. These conversations don't need to be lengthy or with large numbers of people; feedback from a small group (typically under ten) is often sufficient. It's also important to run quick experiments to test your ideas. For instance, if you're considering selling silver wigs, get samples of various wigs and gather customer feedback before placing a large order.

The key principle is to assume nothing and test everything. You can quickly validate your ideas by speaking directly with potential customers to understand their thoughts, needs, challenges, and the solutions they envision.

How to Conduct Customer Interviews

Having established the importance of not making assumptions, the next step is to conduct effective customer interviews. Here's a structured approach:

1. **Define your objective:** Determine the specific information you want to gather. Examples include validating a problem, testing an idea, understanding behaviors, or identifying buying triggers. Be specific (e.g., "Do people experience problem X?" or "Would they pay for solution Y?").

2. **Identify your target audience:** Define the specific group of people you want to talk to. For example, if your target audience is small inn or motel operators with fewer than 20 rooms, focus your outreach on this group. Create a customer persona or segment to guide your outreach and ensure you're speaking with relevant individuals. Use the vocabulary of your target audience when you present your solution.

3. **Prepare your questions:** Avoid leading or yes/no questions. Instead, use open-ended questions like:
   - "Tell me about the last time you experienced X."
   - "How are you currently solving problem Y?"
   - "What do you wish existed that doesn't, and how would it make your life easier?"

Keep the conversation natural and flexible to encourage participants to share insights you may not have anticipated. Open-ended questions help you learn more.

4. **Recruit participants:** Reach out through relevant channels such as online forms, groups, customer lists, or referrals. Consider offering a small incentive (e.g., a gift card or voucher) to show appreciation for their time.

5. **Conduct the interview:** Begin with a brief, warm introduction, explaining who you are, why you're conducting the interview, and that it's not a sales pitch. The primary goal is to listen (80% of the time) rather than talk (20% of the time). Encourage participants to share their experiences and delve deeper when they express frustration, describe workarounds, or show strong emotions. Record the interview (with permission) or take detailed notes to capture as much information as possible.

6. **Analyze the insights:** Look for patterns in the feedback, such as recurring pain points, common language, desires, and behaviors. Cluster these insights into themes like unmet needs, broken workflows, price sensitivity, and product availability. Use these themes to validate or invalidate your initial assumptions and refine your proposed solution.

7. **Act on the findings:** Revise your idea, product, or pitch based on the feedback you receive. Don't treat the interviews as a mere formality; use the insights to drive meaningful changes. Repeat the interview process periodically to continuously refine your understanding of the market and customer needs.

By following these steps, you can gain a strong understanding of customer needs, pain points, and opportunities. Remember to conduct interviews regularly, especially in dynamic markets where customer preferences can change rapidly.

Honest Feedback

To get the most out of conversations with potential customers, you need to prioritize getting honest feedback.

- **Focus on their problems, not your solutions:** Encourage them to talk about their challenges and needs. This is not the time to pitch your product.
- **Focus on past behavior, not opinions:** Ask about what they *have done*, not what they *would do*. If someone says they would buy a product, ask why they haven't bought existing alternatives.
- **Avoid leading questions:** Don't bias their responses with your own ideas or hopes. Instead of asking, "Wouldn't it be great if...?" ask, "How do you currently handle X?"
- **Use neutral framing:** Position the conversation as an opportunity to learn, not a sales pitch. For example, you could say, "I'm trying to understand how people deal with X problem. I'd love to hear how you handle it so I don't build the wrong thing."
- **Listen more, talk less:** Prioritize understanding their perspective.
- **Pre-sell or test commitments:** Gauge their genuine interest by asking for concrete actions, such as signing up for an email list or a waitlist, or indicating how many units they might pre-order and at what price.

Interviewing a small sample of 5 to 10 people initially can yield significant insights and reveal common patterns.

Mistakes to Avoid

Here are some common mistakes to avoid when talking to potential customers:

- **Talking too much about your idea:** The focus should be on the customer's needs and problems.
- **Asking if people like your idea:** Early feedback tends to be polite but not always accurate. Gauge true interest by asking about pricing and purchase intent.
- **Ignoring red flags:** Pay close attention to negative feedback or hesitations. These can reveal critical issues.
- **Interviewing friends:** Friends may provide biased feedback to support you. Talk to people who represent your actual target market; they will provide the most honest and useful feedback because they experience the problem you are trying to solve.

PART 3

NARROWING DOWN AND TESTING YOUR BEST IDEAS

Ranking and Selecting Your Top Business Ideas

T his chapter provides a structured approach to ranking and selecting your most promising business ideas using a comprehensive scoring system. We will delve into a six-table process designed to help you systematically assess your potential ventures, ensuring that the ideas you ultimately pursue align with your skills, passions, and long-term objectives. This chapter aims to provide you with a robust framework, minimizing the risk of pursuing ventures that are misaligned with your personal strengths and aspirations.

A Simple Scoring System for Evaluating Ideas

This evaluation process involves completing six key tables to systematically assess your potential ventures. Each table plays a crucial role in narrowing down your options and focusing your efforts on the ideas with the highest probability of success and personal fulfillment. By the end of this process, you'll have a clear understanding of which ideas warrant further exploration and development.

Module 1: Self-Assessment - Understanding Your Foundation

Table 1: Skills, Passions, and Interests (Appendix)

- **Objective:** To identify your core strengths, inherent talents, and what genuinely motivates and excites you. This foundational step is critical because it ensures that your business endeavors are built upon a bedrock of competence and enthusiasm. A business that leverages your strengths and passions is more likely to be sustainable and enjoyable in the long run.

- **Action:**
  - ◊ In the appendix, create a detailed list of your skills and abilities. For each skill, rate your proficiency on a scale of 1 to 10. Don't limit yourself – if needed, feel free to include more than 10 items to capture the full range

of your capabilities. Consider both hard skills (e.g., coding, accounting) and soft skills (e.g., communication, leadership).

◊ Separately, create a list of your passions and interests. These are the activities, subjects, or areas that you find intrinsically rewarding and engaging. Include anything that sparks your curiosity, brings you joy, or makes you feel energized.

Table 1: Listing skills, passions and interests

What I am great/good at doing:	Effectiveness on a 1-10 scale (10 being highest)
1. Developing new business in emerging and existing markets	10
2. Selling anything to customers	9
3. Creating an understandable user experience and interface	7
4. Managing small teams	6
5. Basic accounting and financial reporting	6
6. Learning new things on my own through exploration and experience	9
What I am passionate about/interested in doing:	Effectiveness on a 1-10 scale (10 being highest)
1. Traveling around the world and experiencing new things	9
2. Vacationing and meeting new people	9
3. Creating new businesses	5
4. Volunteering at homeless shelters and food banks	8
5. Creating music	4
6. Writing	3
7. Making Youtube and Tiktok videos	6

Table 2: Prioritizing Your Strengths and Interests

- **Objective:** To rank your skills and interests in order of importance and proficiency, allowing you to focus on your most valuable assets and deepest sources of motivation. This prioritization helps to ensure that your business idea aligns with what you do best and what you care about most.

- **Action:**
  ◊ Take the comprehensive lists you created in Table 1 and rank them from your highest-rated skills/most intense interests to your lowest. This involves a comparative assessment of each item relative to the others.

  ◊ If two items have the same rating, force rank them by considering which you'd prioritize or which feels more significant to your overall goals and happiness. Think of it as assigning fractional values (e.g., 9.2 vs. 9.1) to differentiate between them.

Table 2. Ranking skills, passions and interests

What I am great/good at, or passionate about/interested in doing:	Score (high to low)
1. Developing new business in emerging and existing markets	10
2. Selling anything to customers	9
3. Traveling around the world and experiencing new things	9
4. Vacationing and meeting new people	9
5. Learning new things on my own through exploration and experience	9
6. Volunteering at homeless shelters and food banks	8
7. Creating an understandable user experience and interface	7
8. Managing small teams	6
9. Basic accounting and financial reporting	6
10. Making Youtube and Tiktok videos	6
11. Creating new businesses	5
12. Creating music	4
13. Writing	3

Module 2: Defining Your Ideal Venture

Table 3: Defining Your Selection Criteria

- **Objective:** To clarify your personal and professional goals for a business venture. This step moves beyond your internal attributes and focuses on the external characteristics of the business itself. It's about defining what you want your business to *do* for you.

- **Action:** Use checkboxes to indicate your priorities. Be honest and realistic about what you truly value in a business:

  ☐ Freedom/Flexibility: Do you prioritize a business that allows you to set your own hours and work location?

  ☐ Wealth: Is your primary goal to generate significant financial returns?

  ☐ Impact: Are you driven by a desire to make a positive difference in the world or in your community?

  ☐ Self-actualization: Do you seek a business that will allow you to fully realize your potential and express your creativity?

  ☐ Others: _____ (Specify any other key priorities)

Consider the following aspects of your ideal business:

- **Location:**

  ☐ Location Independent: Can you operate this business from anywhere in the world?

  ☐ Occasional Visits: Does the business require you to be present in a specific location periodically?

  ☐ Fixed Location: Does the business necessitate a physical presence, such as an office or retail space?

- **Scalability:**

  - ☐ Lifestyle Plan: Is the business intended to provide a comfortable income and support a desired lifestyle, without necessarily growing very large?
  - ☐ Stable with Cash Flow: Are you seeking a business with predictable and consistent revenue, even if growth is moderate?
  - ☐ High Growth: Are you aiming for a business with the potential for rapid and substantial expansion?

- **Risk Tolerance:** (Refer to previous chapter's evaluation for a detailed assessment of your comfort level with risk)

  ☐ Low

  ☐ Medium

  ☐ High

- **Time Element:**

  ☐ Full-time

  ☐ Part-time

  ☐ Side Gig

  ☐ Ad Hoc: Does the work come in bursts, requiring you to dedicate time as needed?

- **Required Skills:** (Review the provided list of typical business skills in the original text and add any other specific skills that you anticipate needing for your potential ventures).

Table 3. Defining selection criteria

Defining Your Selection Criteria		
What do you want?	[X]	Freedom / Flexibility
	[X]	Wealth
	[ ]	Impact
	[ ]	Self Actualisation
	[ ]	Other : _____
The location of the business?	[X]	No location
	[ ]	In the Area (permanence not required)
	[ ]	Fixed Location
Scalability requirement is	[X]	Supporting my lifestyle
	[ ]	Stable cash flow; some growth
	[ ]	High Growth
Risk tolerance is	[ ]	Low
	[X]	Medium
	[ ]	High
Required time commitment	[ ]	Full time
	[X]	Part-time
	[ ]	Evening/weekends
	[ ]	Adhoc
Money to be invested	[ ]	No money
	[X]	Some money
	[ ]	Other people's money

Module 3: Idea Generation and Initial Assessment

Table 4: Listing Ideas and Initial Interest

- **Objective:** To brainstorm a wide range of business ideas and record them, along with your initial level of interest in each. The goal here is quantity over quality in the initial stage – get as many ideas down on paper as possible.

- **Action:**
  - ◊ List every business idea that comes to mind, regardless of how feasible or polished they may seem at this point. Don't censor yourself; the more ideas you generate, the greater your chances of finding a truly exceptional one.
  - ◊ For each idea, briefly describe the core problem it solves or the unmet need it addresses. Then, outline your potential solution – how would your business solve this problem or satisfy this need?
  - ◊ Rate your initial level of interest in pursuing each idea on a scale of 1 to 10. This reflects your gut feeling about the idea's potential and your personal enthusiasm for it. If you haven't yet developed a solution for an idea, leave the "Level of Interest" blank.

Table 4. Listing ideas & evaluation

Idea / Problem	Solution	Rate your level of interest in this idea (1-10; 10 is high)
1. Fleet Tracker for small delivery businesses as you want to know where trucks/buses/bikes are 24/7	Low-cost GPS + dashboard to track truck/bus/bike fleets	5
2. "Try Before You Fly" is needed to virtually see the hotel rooms you might want to rent so it does not upset your vacation	Platform that aggregates 3D hotel room walkthroughs with real-time availability to avoid "buying" wrong rooms	8
3. People need short-term storage facilities when they are between rental properties, or their new place cannot accommodate everything they have	Acquire or build a small local self-storage facility, and improve operations via software and more responsive customer service	9
4. Vertical job board for climate-tech roles because these jobs are difficult to find and aggregate	Curated listings, hiring support, and candidate communities focused on climate startups via a website	6
5. Hotels remain expensive and subpar when you take a vacation as a family, especially in new countries	Buy and/or build out a portfolio of rental units to accommodate travelers that want a "home away from home"	10

Module 4: Refining and Prioritizing Ideas

Table 5: Ranking Top Three Ideas

- **Objective:** To identify your most promising ideas based on your initial assessment of their potential and your personal interest in them. This step begins the process of narrowing down your options to a manageable number.

- **Action:**
  ◊ Rank the ideas you listed in Table 4 based on your "Level of Interest" score, from highest to lowest. This creates a prioritized list of your most intriguing concepts.

  ◊ If any ideas have the same score, force rank them by considering factors such as their long-term potential, alignment with your values, and overall feasibility.

  ◊ Focus your attention on your top three ranked ideas. These are the ideas that warrant further investigation and development, including the crucial step of gathering customer feedback, which we will discuss in the next stage.

Table 5. Ranking ideas

Idea / Problem	Solution	Rank ideas from highest interest level to lowest
1. Hotels remain expensive and subpar when you take a vacation as a family, especially in new countries	Buy and/or build out a portfolio of rental units to accommodate travelers that want a "home away from home"	10
2. People need short-term storage facilities when they are between rental properties, or their new place cannot accommodate everything they have	Acquire or build a small local self-storage facility, and improve operations via software and more responsive customer service	9
3. "Try Before You Fly" is needed to virtually see the hotel rooms you might want to rent so it does not upset your vacation	Platform that aggregates 3D hotel room walkthroughs with real-time availability to avoid "buying" wrong rooms	8
4. Vertical job board for climate-tech roles because these jobs are difficult to find and aggregate	Curated listings, hiring support, and candidate communities focused on climate startups via a website	6
5. Fleet Tracker for small delivery businesses as you want to know where trucks/buses/bikes are 24/7	Low-cost GPS + dashboard to track truck/bus/bike fleets	5

Module 5: Comprehensive Evaluation

Table 6: Evaluation Against Skills, Passion, Interest, and Selection Criteria

- **Objective:** To systematically match your top three ideas against your self-assessment (Tables 1 and 2) and your defined selection criteria (Table 3). This comprehensive evaluation helps you determine which ideas are the best fit for you, considering both your personal attributes and your business aspirations.

- **Action:** This table serves as a comparative tool, aligning each of your top three ideas with the information you've compiled in Tables 1, 2, and 3. It allows you to see, side-by-side, how well each idea leverages your strengths, aligns with your passions, and fulfills your desired business criteria. This process will provide you with a more objective and data-driven perspective on which ideas are most likely to lead to success and satisfaction.

Table 6. Evaluation of ideas against skills, passions, interest and selection criteria

Idea

Starting a group of AirBnB rentals focused on people that decide to vacation in major cities during peak periods. Expectation is that the lack of lodging options at those times would increase the revenue to 3X during these peak periods ensuring that all revenues are made in the 1-2 months of peak business visits or tourism.

CAPABILITIES ASSESSMENT

Skills Required for Idea to Succeed	Needs	I have	Gap
Product			0
Sales	10	5	5
Sector experience/understanding	10	10	0
Technology			0
Relationships	10	6	4
Distribution	10	6	4
Capital	10	5	5
Legal / Compliance	10	10	0
Competitive Positioning	10	10	0
Management			0
SUBTOTAL	**70**		**18**
			26%

FIT ASSESSMENT

Things I Want vs What Idea Offers	Offers	I want	Gap
Freedom / Flexibility	7	10	0
Wealth	5	10	0
Impact			0
Self Actualisation			0
Other : _____			0
No location	8	10	0
In the Area (permanence not required)			0
Fixed Location			0
Supporting my lifestyle	10	10	0
Stable cash flow; some growth			0
High Growth			0
Low			0
Medium	10	10	0
High			0
Full time			0
Part-time	10	10	0
Evening/weekends			0
Adhoc			0
No money			0
Some money	10	2	8
Other people's money			0
SUB-TOTAL	**60**		**8**
			13%
TOTAL	**130**		**26**
			20%

Avoiding Over-Analysis: Trust Your Gut

After completing Table 6 and carefully reviewing the data, take a step back and consider your intuition. While the tables provide a valuable framework for evaluation, they don't capture the full complexity of human decision-making. If one of the lower-ranked ideas strongly resonates with you on a gut level, take the time to explore why. Sometimes, your underlying passion, your subconscious awareness of market opportunities, or a deep-seated sense of "rightness" can be powerful indicators that the numbers don't fully capture.

Don't dismiss this internal voice; it might be guiding you towards a more fulfilling and ultimately more successful path. Instead of trying to force the numbers to align with your feelings, take time for introspection to understand the reasons behind your preferences. Are there personal values, emotional considerations, or past experiences that are influencing your judgment? By acknowledging and exploring these factors, you can make a more informed and authentic decision about which business idea to pursue.

8

Starting – The 28-Day Challenge

This chapter provides a 28-day plan to guide you from generating your initial idea to launching your new company. This structured sequence will help you validate your business idea and effectively prepare for entering the market.

The 28-Day Challenge

By following this plan, you should be ready to launch your company within 28 days. While the pace of progress may vary, this framework will ensure a thorough and methodical approach to getting started.

Day 1: Complete Tables 1 and 2

- Begin by identifying your skills, passions, and interests using Table 1, and then prioritize them in Table 2.
- It's recommended that you revisit Table 1 on Day 2 to make any necessary adjustments after your initial reflection.

Day 2: Complete Table 3

- Next, define your selection criteria in Table 3, carefully considering your personal and professional goals.
- To make the most informed decisions, use your responses from Tables 1 and 2 to guide you through this process.

Days 3-16: Complete Table 4

- During this period, generate a list of potential business ideas, along with their corresponding problems and solutions, in Table 4.
- Developing and refining your ideas may take time, so allow yourself ample space for this process.
- For each idea, assign a level of interest on a scale of 1 to 10.

Days 17-25: Complete Table 5

- Complete Table 5 by force-ranking your top three ideas.
- For each of these top three ideas, conduct interviews with 3 to 10 prospective customers.
  - ◊ This step is crucial for validating your ideas by understanding actual customer needs.

◊ Based on the feedback you receive, you can then decide to:
- Keep the idea on your list.
- Replace it with another idea.
- Proceed with only one or two ideas that show the most promise.

Day 26: Complete Table 6

- Use Table 6 to evaluate your ideas.
- This table allows you to integrate your skills, passions, interests, and selection criteria to help you choose the most suitable business idea.

Day 27: Complete Table 7

- Perform a financial assessment of your chosen idea using Table 7.
- This assessment will help you determine your business's potential profitability.

Day 28: Start!

- Finalize your plan, set your targets, and launch your venture with confidence.

Assessing Profitability Models

Simple Financial Assessment

Table 7 provides a framework for evaluating your idea's profitability on a unit basis.

- Begin by estimating the number of units, whether physical or non-physical, that you can realistically sell.
- Then, determine both the unit price and the cost per unit, including the value of your time if applicable.
- Calculate your estimated monthly revenue using the following formula: Unit Price x Estimated Units Sold.
- To determine your net profit, you'll need to account for all monthly expenses, including:
  ◊ Personnel costs
  ◊ Rent
  ◊ Equipment lease payments
  ◊ Transportation expenses
  ◊ Loan repayment expenses
  ◊ Utility costs
  ◊ Marketing and sales expenses
  ◊ Distribution costs
  ◊ Any other relevant operating expenses

- Finally, calculate your net profit by subtracting your total expenses from your total revenue: Revenue - Expenses.

This assessment will indicate whether your idea has the potential for positive unit economics and is financially viable.

Table 7. Simple financial assessment of business

		Monthly
Price at which you can you sell 1 unit of what you have	A	400
How much does it cost to produce 1 unit	B	150
How many units will you sell in one month	C	34
Gross Revenue	A*C	13,600
Cost of Sales	B*C	5,100
Gross Profit	(A-B)*C	8,500
Expenses (for 1 month)		
People		1,200
Rent		-
Leases		-
Transportation		-
Loan payment		1,500
Utilities		250
Sales & Marketing		1,200
Distribution / Partnerships		-
Other		-
Total	D	4,150
Net Profit (pre-tax)	[(A-B)*C] - D	4,350
		32%

Key Points:

- **Negative Unit Economics:** If your costs consistently exceed your selling price, this will significantly hinder your business's growth and long-term sustainability.
- **Growth vs. Profitability:** While some businesses may prioritize initial growth over immediate profitability, maintaining positive unit economics is crucial for your long-term success.

Differentiating Between a Business Owner and an Entrepreneur

9

This chapter explores the distinction between a business owner and an entrepreneur. It's positioned later in this book because understanding these categories is most valuable after you've engaged in self-discovery and determined where you naturally align.

Key Differences: Business Owner vs. Entrepreneur

A fundamental difference exists between a business owner and an entrepreneur. Business owners typically prioritize stability, profitability, and sustainable operations, focusing heavily on efficient operations and profit generation. If your responses to the previous challenges indicate a preference for these qualities, you may be inclined towards business ownership, particularly in industries where operational optimization is key.

Entrepreneurs, on the other hand, often emphasize innovation, scalability, and disruption. Their ventures may disrupt existing markets, creating substantial shifts as markets move towards their new offerings. The central question is: Which path resonates most with you? Your choices in the preceding chapters will provide insights into this.

Business Owner

We'll begin by examining the business owner profile, starting with mindset and then moving on to the requirements for success.

Business Owner Mindset

The business owner's mindset involves a transition from self-employment to true business ownership.

- **From Self-Employed to Business Owner:** The old mindset is characterized by the belief that "I am the business, and if I don't work, nothing happens." The new mindset recognizes, "I own a business that should operate without my constant micromanagement." This shift requires building systems, delegating tasks, and focusing on scaling operations and the team, rather than merely trading time for money.

- **From Revenue Focus to Profit Focus:** The old mindset equates success with more sales. The new mindset understands that "more profit equals success." This involves cutting unnecessary costs, pricing strategically, and meticulously tracking margins.

- **From Doing Everything to Owning the Vision:** The old mindset is characterized by the need to handle all key tasks personally. The new mindset recognizes that the job is to lead, not to do. This entails hiring or outsourcing to address weaknesses and concentrating on high-impact decisions.

- **From Short-Term Hustle to Long-Term Equity:** The old mindset focuses on grinding now for future rewards. The new mindset focuses on building an asset that grows in value by investing in branding, systems, and customer loyalty for lasting value.

- **From Competing on Price to Competing on Value:** The old mindset centers around being the cheapest option. The new mindset focuses on competing based on quality, service, and uniqueness. The action here is to differentiate your brand, confidently raise prices, and attract better clients.

- **From Fear of Losing Customers to Focusing on Ideal Customers:** The old mindset is characterized by an inability to say no to any customer, driven by the need for every sale. The new mindset involves firing bad clients and focusing on the best ones by setting boundaries, raising prices, and specializing in a niche.

- **From Linear Growth to Leveraged Growth:** The old mindset equates growth with working harder. The new mindset sees growth as working smarter through automation, partnerships, and scaling. This involves using available tools, affiliates, and recurring revenue models.

- **From Avoiding Risk to Managing Risk:** The old mindset involves waiting until everything is perfect. The new mindset embraces taking smart risks and adjusting rapidly by testing ideas cheaply, failing quickly, and iterating.

- **From Emotional Spending to Strategic Investing:** The old mindset involves spending based on feelings of confidence. The new mindset dictates that every dollar spent must generate a return, which requires measuring ROI on marketing tools and hires.

- **From Solo Operator to CEO Mindset:** The old mindset identifies with a specific role (e.g., technician, consultant, shop owner). The new mindset is, "I'm the CEO, and my role is strategy and leadership." This shift requires thinking like an executive, not just a worker.

Ultimately, the business owner's mindset shifts towards viewing the business as a machine designed to operate efficiently.

Business Owner Requirements for Success

Here are some key requirements for a business owner's success:

1. **Financial Discipline:** Understand cash flow, profit margins, and budgeting; avoid overspending and manage debt wisely; reinvest profits strategically for growth.

2. **Operational Efficiency:** Build systems and processes to streamline operations; focus on productivity and cost control; utilize automation and delegation effectively.

3. **Customer Focus:** Prioritize customer satisfaction and retention; actively listen to feedback and adapt offerings; build strong relationships for repeat business.

4. **Decision-Making Under Uncertainty:** Make quick, informed decisions with incomplete information; balance risks and rewards pragmatically; learn from mistakes.

5. **Leadership and Team Management:** Hire the right people and foster a strong company culture; delegate effectively without micromanaging; motivate employees and resolve conflicts.

6. **Sales and Negotiation Skills:** Effectively sell products and services; negotiate favorable deals with suppliers, partners, and clients; understand pricing strategies and value propositions.

7. **Adaptability and Market Awareness:** Stay updated on industry trends and competition; pivot business models when necessary; anticipate changes in technology, regulations, and customer behavior.

8. **Problem-Solving and Resourcefulness:** Find creative solutions with limited resources; handle crises calmly (e.g., supply chain issues, customer complaints); turn obstacles into opportunities.

9. **Time Management and Focus:** Prioritize high-impact tasks; avoid busy work and distractions; maintain discipline; balance work and personal life to prevent burnout.

10. **Resilience and Stress Management:** Handle setbacks without losing motivation; maintain composure under pressure; keep a long-term perspective during difficult times.

11. **Networking and Relationship Building:** Build trust with customers, suppliers, and mentors; leverage partnerships for growth; engage with industry groups and local business communities.

12. **Legal and Compliance Awareness:** Understand basic business laws, taxes, contracts, and employment rules; avoid legal pitfalls; consult experts (accountants, lawyers) and liaise with regulators as needed.

13. **Branding and Marketing Savvy:** Position the business effectively in the market; use digital marketing, social media, and SEO effectively; build a strong reputation and trust in both online and offline spheres.

14. **Long-Term Vision with Short-Term Execution:** Plan for future growth while managing daily operations; set achievable milestones and track progress; avoid complacency and continuously seek improvements.

15. **Ownership Mindset:** Take full responsibility for successes and failures; think like an investor, not just an operator; seek to increase business value.

In conclusion, successful business owners don't need to be exceptionally gifted; they simply need to master the fundamentals, remain adaptable, and execute consistently. Many of these skills can be acquired through experience and mentorship.

Entrepreneur

Now, let's turn our attention to the entrepreneur's mindset.

Entrepreneur Mindset

The entrepreneur's mindset is characterized by:

- **Resilience and Grit:** The ability to bounce back from failure and persevere through significant setbacks with long-term persistence.
- **Vision and Strategic Thinking:** Possessing clear long-term goals, the ability to identify opportunities others miss, and the adaptability to pivot without losing sight of the mission.
- **Strong Work Ethic:** A willingness to exert considerable effort, particularly in the early stages, and self-discipline to maintain productivity without external pressure.
- **Problem-Solving Mindset:** A focus on solutions rather than just problems, with creativity and resourcefulness in overcoming obstacles.
- **Calculated Risk Tolerance:** Comfort with uncertainty and calculated risk-taking, as opposed to recklessness; a willingness to make smart bets.
- **Customer-Centric Approach:** A deep understanding of customer pain points and a strong commitment to delivering genuine value, not just making sales.
- **Basic Financial Literacy:** A foundational understanding of cash flow, profit margins, and investment, with the ability to

manage budgets and make sound financial decisions.

- **Sales and Persuasion Skills:** The ability to sell a vision to customers, investors, employees, and other stakeholders, along with strong negotiation and communication skills.

- **Leadership and Team Building:** The capacity to inspire and motivate others, delegate effectively, and hire individuals who are more skilled.

- **Continuous Learning and Adaptability:** Staying updated on industry trends and acquiring new skills, with openness to feedback and a willingness to discard outdated methods.

- **Emotional Intelligence:** The ability to manage stress and handle rejection, maintain strong relationships, and effectively read people—a crucial skill for networking and hiring.

- **Self-Awareness and Humility:** Recognizing personal strengths and weaknesses, seeking help when needed, and learning from mistakes instead of assigning blame.

- **Bias for Action:** A tendency to execute quickly rather than overthinking, with a willingness to refine strategies as you proceed.

- **Networking and Relationship Building:** Building a strong support system of mentors, partners, and peers, recognizing that opportunities often arise through these connections.

- **Passion and Purpose:** A deep belief in the venture's mission, fueling persistence and prioritizing purpose alongside profit.

Requirements for Success for an Entrepreneur

An entrepreneur's success hinges on several key shifts in perspective and approach:

1. **From Fixed to Growth Mindset:** A fixed mindset assumes that skills and intelligence are static, while a growth mindset embraces learning, adaptation, and views failure as feedback. The shift involves seeing challenges as opportunities for growth, not as threats.

2. **From Perfectionism to Progress Over Perfection:** Waiting for the perfect product or moment leads to missed opportunities. Entrepreneurs must embrace launching, iterating, and improving based on real-world feedback, embodying a minimum viable product (MVP) mindset.

3. **From Scarcity to Abundance Thinking:** A scarcity mindset fosters fierce competition and the hoarding of ideas and resources. An abundance mindset recognizes limitless opportunities and values collaboration over competition. The shift involves focusing on value creation rather than fearing others' success.

4. **From Employee to Owner Thinking:** Employees trade time for money, while entrepreneurs build systems for leverage. The shift involves prioritizing scalability, delegation, and passive income streams.

5. **From Short-Term to Long-Term Vision:** Avoid pursuing quick wins that don't align with long-term objectives. Instead, invest in relationships, branding, and sustainable growth.

6. **From Pure Failure to Intelligent Risk-Taking:** View failure as data, not defeat. Successful entrepreneurs fail repeatedly, learning to take calculated risks, act quickly, and pivot when necessary.

7. **From Solo Hero to Team Builder:** Attempting to do everything alone limits growth. The shift involves hiring or partnering with individuals whose skills complement your weaknesses.

8. **From "I Know It All" to Constant Learning:** Markets evolve, and stagnation can destroy businesses. The shift involves a relentless pursuit of knowledge through reading, networking, and seeking mentors.

9. **From Emotional to Strategic Decision-Making:** Allowing fear, pride, or impatience to dictate choices leads to errors. The shift involves using data, logic, and long-term impact as filters for decisions.

10. **From Making Money to Creating Value:** Recognize that profit is a consequence of solving real problems and meeting customer needs. The shift involves focusing on the customer and trusting that financial success will follow.

Which are You?

Both business owners and entrepreneurs play vital roles in the economy, but they approach their ventures with distinct mindsets and priorities. Business owners excel at creating stable, profitable enterprises through efficient operations and strategic management. Entrepreneurs, on the other hand, drive innovation and growth by embracing risk, disruption, and scalability. Your self-discovery journey will determine which path aligns best with your strengths, passions, and goals.

Ultimately, success in either role depends less on innate talent and more on cultivating the appropriate mindset and acquiring key skills. Whether you choose to build a well-oiled business machine or disrupt industries with innovative solutions, continuous learning, adaptability, and a commitment to execution are essential.

CONCLUSION

The Journey,
Not the Classification

This book intentionally avoided asking you to categorize yourself from the outset. Instead, it guided you through a process of self-discovery. If you had been asked to choose between "entrepreneur" and "business owner" at the beginning, you might have made a superficial choice. Some might have gravitated towards the perceived excitement of being an entrepreneur, while others might have preferred the stability of business ownership.

By not providing those initial boxes, you were encouraged to first engage in internal reflection, followed by an external assessment. You then used this information to determine your natural inclinations. Throughout this process, your inherent traits began to emerge, making it difficult to ignore your true preferences.

Chapter 9 allows you to reflect on whether you identify more with the entrepreneurial or business owner mindset. It's important to remember that these are not mutually exclusive categories. Many people begin as entrepreneurs and evolve into business owners, while others might start as business owners and later embrace an entrepreneurial opportunity. These factors place you on a spectrum rather than in a fixed category.

This book has equipped you with the knowledge and tools to embark on an exciting journey of business creation. You've explored your strengths, evaluated opportunities, and gained the confidence to take the next step. As you stand at the threshold of turning your ideas into reality, remember that the path ahead is filled with possibilities.

The challenges of developing your idea lie ahead, and the fact that you've embarked on this quest should be both exciting and exhilarating. Embrace the challenges, learn from every experience, and persevere with passion and determination. Your journey towards ownership and building your dreams is about to begin.

I wish you the best of luck as you pursue your ownership and business-building goals. May your efforts be met with success, fulfillment, and the realization of your vision.

ABOUT THE AUTHOR

W ith a distinguished career spanning over three decades, Ike Eze stands at the intersection of entrepreneurship, investment, and thought leadership in the global technology landscape. Ike's journey began with a solid technical foundation, earning a BS in Mechanical Engineering from San Francisco State University, followed by an MBA in Finance and Strategic Management from the prestigious Wharton School at the University of Pennsylvania.

Ike's early professional years were shaped by impactful roles at world-renowned corporations such as Boston Consulting Group (BCG), Bechtel, and AT&T, where he honed his expertise in strategic management and large-scale technical operations. Driven by an entrepreneurial spirit, he went on to found and build three successful Silicon Valley tech startups, navigating the demanding path from inception and capital formation to growth and exit. This hands-on experience provided him with invaluable insights into the challenges and triumphs faced by founders and business owners.

Over the past two decades, Ike transitioned from building companies to investing in them, focusing his keen eye for innovation on technology startups. A decade ago, recognizing the untapped potential of emerging markets, he expanded his investment portfolio to include dynamic ventures across Africa, Asia, and beyond. Today, Ike is a trusted advisor and board member for both private and public companies, leveraging his deep industry knowledge to guide organizations through growth, transformation, and market entry.

A passionate advocate for entrepreneurship, Ike has mentored countless aspiring founders and business owners. Throughout his career, he encountered a recurring question: How does one pinpoint the right idea to start or buy a business? In response, Ike developed a practical, actionable methodology to help entrepreneurs and business owners discover and validate business ideas—a framework that forms the foundation of his acclaimed book.

Beyond his investment and advisory work, Ike is an accomplished writer and thought leader. He has contributed as a guest writer for the Huffington Post and published numerous articles on entrepreneurship, innovation, and emerging markets. His latest book distills decades of experience into a clear roadmap for anyone seeking to embark on their own entrepreneurial journey.

Whether as an investor, board member, advisor, or author, Ike Eze remains dedicated to empowering the next generation of entrepreneurs to turn ideas into thriving businesses.

Did you enjoy the book? Consider leaving
a review by scanning the QR code below or
visiting the link

Write a review

www.thefounderfit.com/review

APPENDIX

Table 1. Listing skills, passions, and interests

What I am great/good at doing:	Effectiveness on a 1-10 scale (10 being highest)
1.	
2.	
3.	
4.	
5.	
6.	
7.	
8.	
9.	
10.	
What I am passionate about/interested in doing:	**Effectiveness on a 1-10 scale (10 being highest)**
1.	
2.	
3.	
4.	
5.	
6.	
7.	
8.	
9.	
10.	

Table 2. Ranking skills, passions, and interests

What I am great/good at, or passionate about/interested in doing:	Score (high to low)
1.	
2.	
3.	
4.	
5.	
6.	
7.	
8.	
9.	
10.	
11.	
12.	
13.	
14.	
15.	
16.	
17.	
18.	
19.	
20.	

Table 3. Defining selection criteria

Defining Your Selection Criteria

What do you want?	☐	Freedom / Flexibility
	☐	Wealth
	☐	Impact
	☐	Self Actualisation
	☐	Other : _____
The location of the business?	☐	No location
	☐	In the Area (permanence not required)
	☐	Fixed Location
Scalability requirement is	☐	Supporting my lifestyle
	☐	Stable cash flow; some growth
	☐	High Growth
Risk tolerance is	☐	Low
	☐	Medium
	☐	High
Required time commitment	☐	Full time
	☐	Part-time
	☐	Evening/weekends
	☐	Adhoc
Money to be invested	☐	No money
	☐	Some money
	☐	Other people's money

Table 4. Listing ideas & evaluation

Idea / Problem	Solution	Rate your level of interest in this idea (1-10; 10 is high)
1.		
2.		
3.		
4.		
5.		
6.		
7.		
8.		
9.		
10.		

Table 5. Ranking ideas

Idea / Problem	Solution	Rank ideas from highest interest level to lowest
1.		
2.		
3.		
4.		
5.		
6.		
7.		
8.		
9.		
10.		

Table 6. Evaluation of ideas against skills, passions, interest and selection criteria

Idea

CAPABILITIES ASSESSMENT

Skills Required for Idea to Succeed	Needs	I have	Gap
Product			
Sales			
Sector experience/understanding			
Technology			
Relationships			
Distribution			
Capital			
Legal / Compliance			
Competitive Positioning			
Management			
SUBTOTAL			

calculate the gap in %

FIT ASSESSMENT

Things I Want vs What Idea Offers	Offers	I want	Gap
Freedom / Flexibility			
Wealth			
Impact			
Self Actualisation			
Other : _____			
No location			
In the Area (permanence not required)			
Fixed Location			
Supporting my lifestyle			
Stable cash flow; some growth			
High Growth			
Low			
Medium			
High			
Full time			
Part-time			
Evening/weekends			
Adhoc			
No money			
Some money			
Other people's money			
SUB-TOTAL			

calculate the gap in %

TOTAL		

calculate the gap in %

Table 7. Simple financial assessment of business

Monthly

Price at which you can you sell 1 unit of what you have	A	
How much does it cost to produce 1 unit	B	
How many units will you sell in 1 month	C	
Gross Revenue	A*C	
Cost of Sales	B*C	
Gross Profit	(A-B)*C	_____

Expenses (for 1 month)

   People

   Rent

   Leases

   Transportation

   Loan payment

   Utilities

   Sales & Marketing

   Distribution / Partnerships

   Others

   Total   D

Net Profit (pre-tax)   [(A-B)*C] - D   _____

profit as % of revenues